ANDREA CAPPELLARI

FIRST BOOK
OF CLASSICAL FLUTE

FLUTE

To access companion recorded accompaniments
online, visit:
www.halleonard.com/mylibrary
Enter Code
1844-2868-0997-0125

ISBN 978-1-5400-5461-6

RICORDI

EXCLUSIVELY DISTRIBUTED BY
HAL•LEONARD®

Visit Hal Leonard Online at
www.halleonard.com

Contact us:
Hal Leonard
7777 West Bluemound Road
Milwaukee, WI 53213
Email: info@halleonard.com

In Europe, contact:
Hal Leonard Europe Limited
42 Wigmore Street
Marylebone, London, W1U 2RN
Email: info@halleonardeurope.com

In Australia, contact:
Hal Leonard Australia Pty. Ltd.
4 Lentara Court
Cheltenham, Victoria, 3192 Australia
Email: info@halleonard.com.au

Andrea Cappellari holds degrees in choral music and choral conducting, music education, and percussion instruments from the Giuseppe Verdi Conservatory in Milan. He is a lecturer at the Giacomo Puccini Higher Institute of Music Studies in Gallarate, Varese, Italy, and at the Candiani-Bausch High School of the Arts in Busto Arizio, Varese, Italy. He teaches training and continuing education courses for teachers and courses in rhythm and ensemble music in French-speaking Switzerland. He is a director of choral and instrumental ensembles, and author of numerous educational publications and collections of children's songs.

In memory of my beloved mother Wanda.

Thanks to Fabiana Colombo, Carlo Torretta

Cover Art by Giuseppe Spada

INTRODUCTION

This collection of composers' melodies intended for the first year of study comes from the teaching experience of Andrea Cappellari.

I am convinced that teaching practices designed for the beginner and a methodology for more direct basic music learning that accompanies traditional pedagogy are needed.

The one hundred melodies all come from compositions by classical composers. They employ a minimum of three to a maximum of eight notes, and arranged for beginning students. They are characterized by the absence of sixteenth notes, using the eighth note as the smallest value. As you continue in the study, the volume presents new positions on the flute with diagonal diagrams—just as the flute is held—which facilitate the study by the beginner. The collection, organized by progressive technical and musical difficulties, can also be used in a small group (with piano and/or another flute).

The fluency, the brevity and the simplicity of the beautiful melodies contained in the *First Book of Classical Flute* also facilitate the study of memorization. This ability, which must be exercised from the first steps on the instrument, will provide a sense of security and stability for the beginner.

Lisa B. Friend
flute teacher at the Conservatoire Stanislao Giacomantonio in Cosenza, Italy

CONTENTS

Section 1. Melodies of 3 Notes

6 G, A, B

Section 2. Melodies of 4 Notes

8 G, A, B, C

Section 3. Melodies of 5 Notes

10 G, A, B, C, D

12 **Section 4. Melodies of 5 Notes**

Section 5. Melodies of 6 Notes

14 G, A, B, C, D, E

Section 6. Melodies of 5 Notes

16 D, E, F-sharp, G, A

17 **Section 7. G-Major Scale**

Section 8. Melodies of 3 Notes

20 F, G, A

Section 9. Melodies of 5 Notes

21 F, G, A, B-flat, C

Section 10. Melodies of 6 Notes

22 E, F, G, A, B-flat, C

23 **Section 11. F-Major Scale**

Section 12. Melodies of 6 Notes

26 F-sharp, G, A, B, C, D

Section 13. Melodies of 5 Notes

28 E, F-sharp, G, A, B

Section 14. Melodies of 5 Notes

30 D, E, F-sharp, G, A

Section 15. Melodies of 4 Notes

32 G, A, B, C

33 **Section 16. C-Major Scale**

37 **Fingering Chart**

39 **Glossary**

MELODIES INDEXED BY COMPOSER

Anonymous
56

Johann Beranek
44

Maternus Beringer
30, 31

Ferdinand Beyer
1, 2, 3, 4, 5, 6, 7, 10, 11,
12, 13, 16, 17, 18, 19, 22,
25, 52, 55, 67, 77, 78

Johannes Brahms
33

Friedrich Burgmüller
100

Dieterich Buxtehude
74

Antonio Caldara
68

André Campra
27

**Marc-Antoine
Charpentier**
41, 63, 73

Arcangelo Corelli
85

Michel Corrette
39

Carl Czerny
24, 58, 65

Anton Diabelli
81

Antonín Dvořák
42

Arthur Foote
61, 82, 83, 86

César Franck
35, 93

Baldassare Galuppi
50, 51

**Giovanni Giacomo
Gastoldi**
79

Ludwig Ernst Gebhardi
64, 71, 96, 97, 98

Christian Geist
29

Mauro Giuliani
75

Charles Gounod
66

Enrique Granados
40

P. B. Gruber
72

George Frideric Handel
23, 87

Winslow Lewis Hayden
36, 70

Michael Haydn
15, 28, 95

Nikolaus Herman
21

Konrad Max Kunz
53, 54, 84, 89, 90, 91

Gustav Lange
94

Franz Liszt
8, 9

Martin Luther
20

Domenico Manzolo
80

Felix Mendelssohn
34

**Wolfgang Amadeus
Mozart**
26, 45, 46, 48, 57, 60

Johann Pachelbel
43

Ignaz Pleyel
76, 92

Nicola Porpora
47, 49

Henry Purcell
59

Johann Rosenmüller
62

Anton Schmoll
14, 37, 38, 88, 99

Franz Schubert
69

Bedřich Smetana
32

1 Melodies of 3 Notes/Rhythmic Values: 𝅝 𝅗𝅮. 𝅗𝅮 𝅘

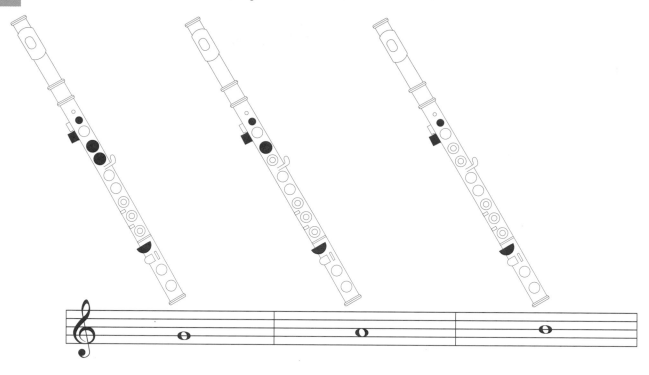

2 Melodies of 4 Notes/Rhythmic Values: o d. d d

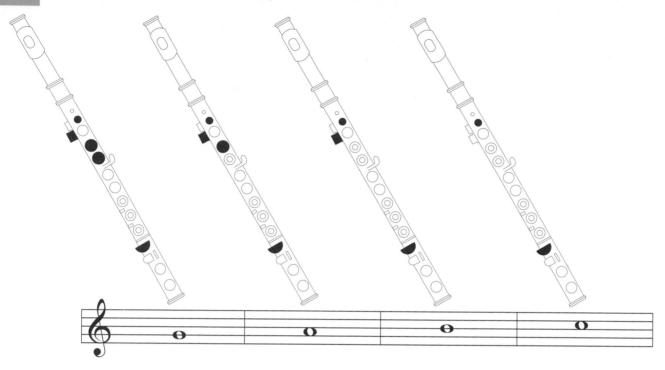

F. LISZT
Ave verum corpus

Lento

9

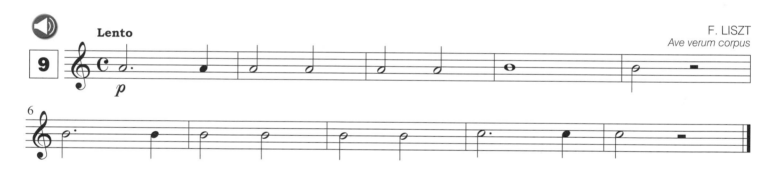

F. BEYER
Op. 101

Moderato

10

F. BEYER
Op. 101

Moderato

11

3 Melodies of 5 Notes/Rhythmic Values: 𝅝 𝅗𝅥. 𝅗𝅥 𝅘𝅥

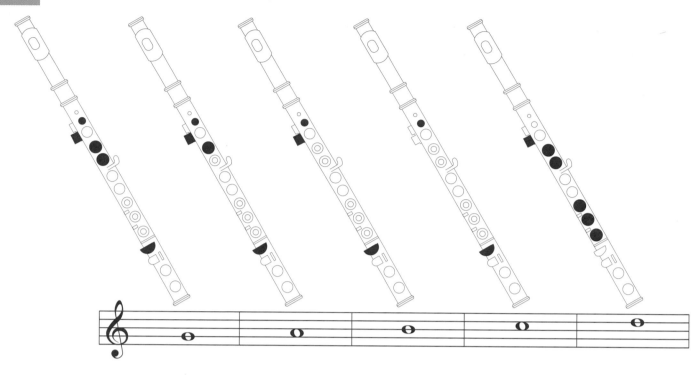

M. LUTHER (1483-1546)
Nun freut euch

N. HERMAN (1500-1560)
Aus meines Herzens Grunde

F. BEYER
Op. 101

G.F. HANDEL (1685-1759)
Sing ye to the Lord (Israel in Aegypt)

Preparatory Exercises

C. CZERNY (1791-1857)
Op. 777

F. BEYER
Op. 101

W.A. MOZART (1756-1791)
Menuetto (Serie 24 n. 58)

A. CAMPRA (1660-1744)
Jubilate Deo

M. HAYDN
Kommt, ihr Christen

C. GEIST (1640-1711)
Verbum caro

5 | Melodies of 6 Notes/Rhythmic Values: from 𝅝 to ♪

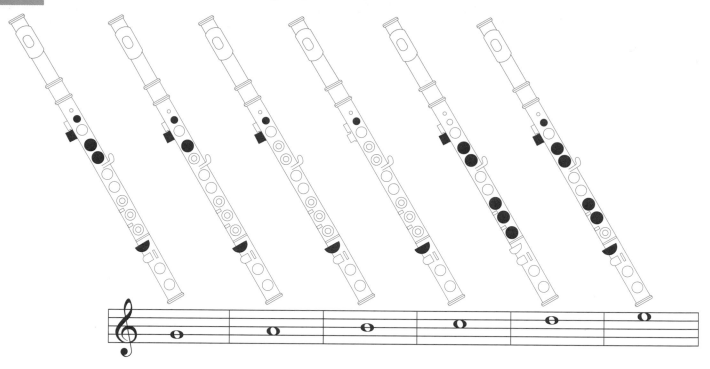

M. BERINGER (1580-1632)
Canon

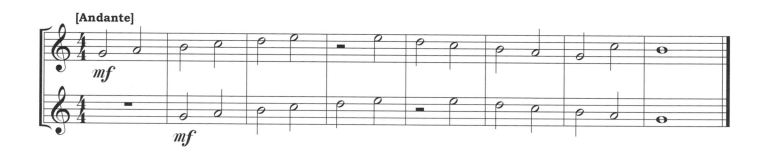

M. BERINGER
Canon

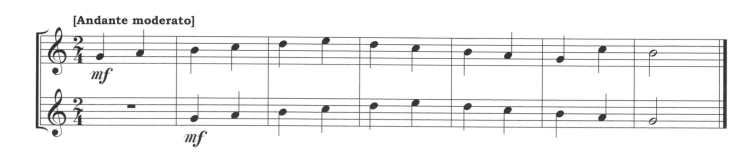

6 Melodies of 5 Notes/Rhythmic Values: from 𝅗𝅥. to ♪

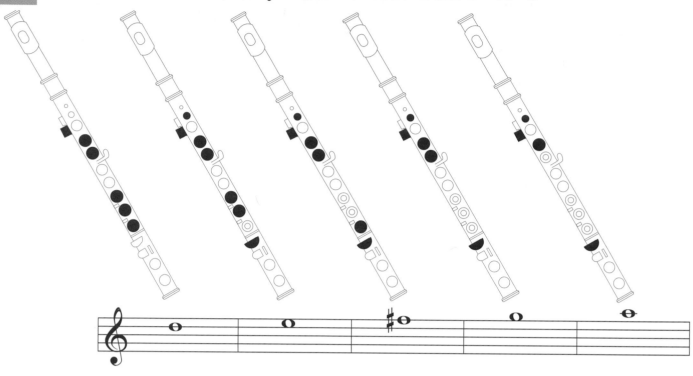

Un poco animato

A. SCHMOLL
Petit Étude

37

𝆏

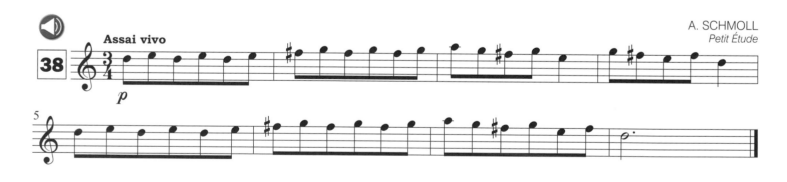

Assai vivo

A. SCHMOLL
Petit Étude

38

𝆏

[Allegretto]

M. CORRETTE (1707-1795)
Menuet allemand

39

𝆐𝆑

7 G-Major Scale

8 Melodies of 3 Notes/Rhythmic Values: 𝅝 𝅗𝅥 ♪

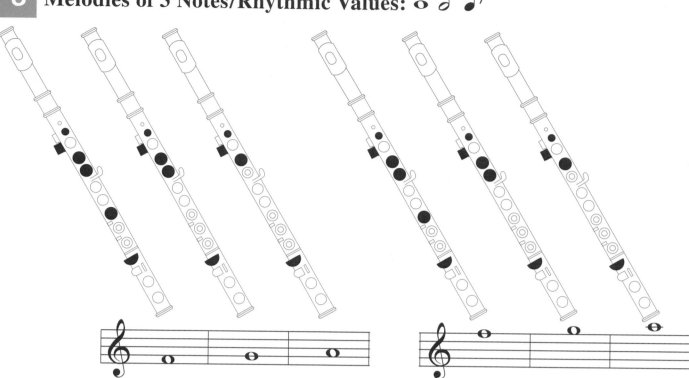

F. BEYER
Op. 101

52 Moderato

mf [2nd time octave higher]

K.M. KUNZ (1812-1875)
Canons Op. 14

53 Moderato

mf

mf

K.M. KUNZ
Canons Op. 14

54 Moderato

mf

mf

9 **Melodies of 5 Notes/Rhythmic Values: from 𝅝 to ♪**

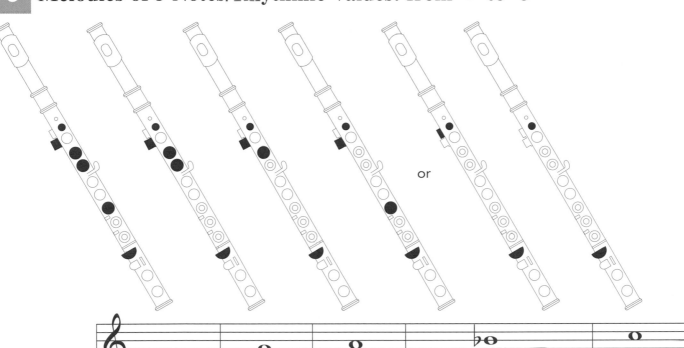

or

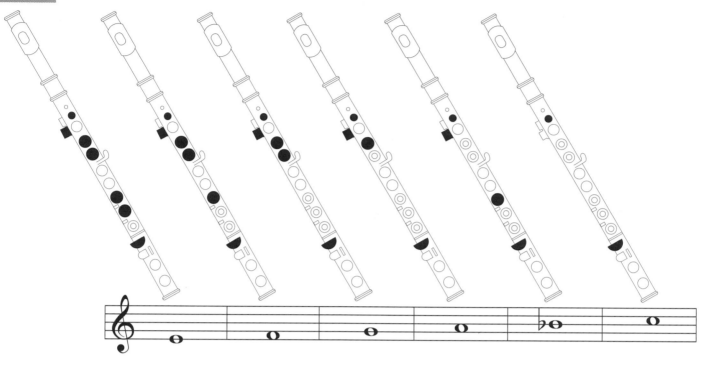

H. PURCELL (1659-1695)
A new Irish tune

59 Moderato

mf

W.A. MOZART
Deutsche Tänze - Serie 11 n. 13

60 [Allegro]

mf

A. FOOTE (1853-1937)
Reverie

61 Andante

p

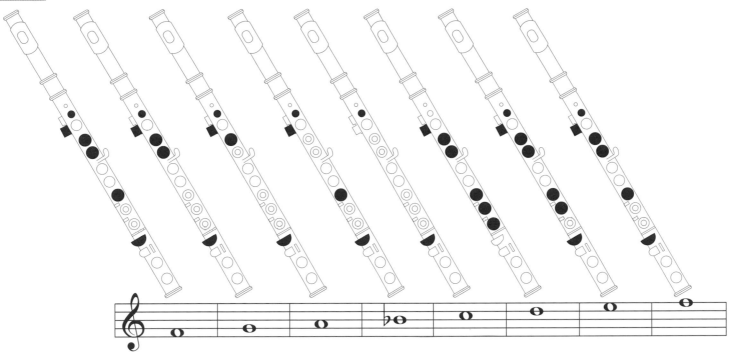

J. ROSENMÜLLER (1619-1684)
Meine Seele harret auf Gott

62 **Presto** *mf*

M.A. CHARPENTIER
Domine Deus (Messe de minuit)

63 **Lento** *p*

L.E. GEBHARDI (1787-1862)
Two-part canon

64 **Moderato** *mf*

FIRST BOOK OF CLASSICAL FLUTE

F. BEYER Op. 101

6 Moderato

F. BEYER Op. 101

7 Moderato

F. LISZT (1811-1886) *Pater noster*

8 Lento

2

D. BUXTEHUDE (1637-1707) Sinfonia: *Du Friedefürst*

M. GIULIANI (1781-1829) Op. 50 n. 1

A. DIABELLI (1781-1858) *Alla turca*

A. FOOTE *A little Waltz*

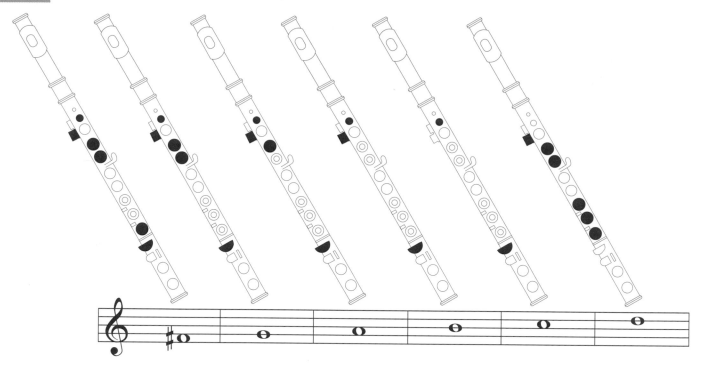

P.B. GRUBER (1759-1796)
Ave Regina coelorum

72 Andante

mf

M.A. CHARPENTIER
Klein Te Deum

73 Andante

mf

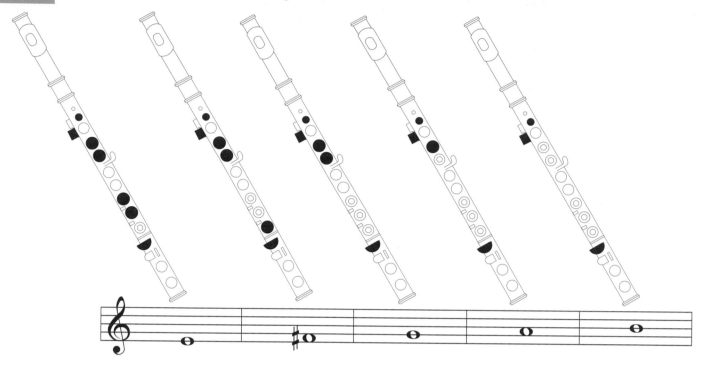

F. BEYER
Op. 101

77 **Allegretto**

p

Fine

D.C. al Fine

F. BEYER
Op. 101

78 **Andante**

mf

G. GASTOLDI (1555-1622)
La cortigiana

79 **[Andante moderato]**

mf

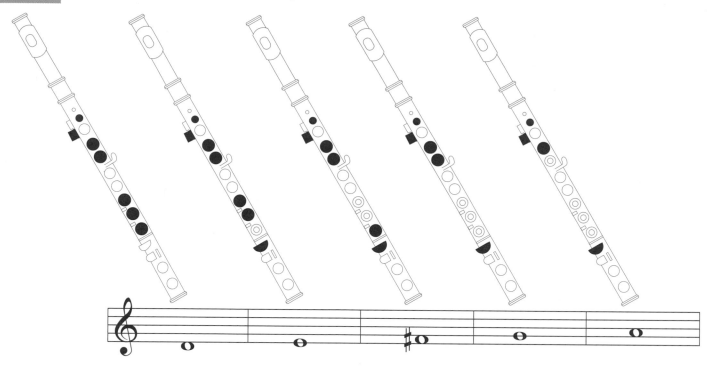

A. FOOTE
Quite contented

K. KUNZ
Canon

I. PLEYEL (1757-1831)
Rondò - Sonatina n. 1

92 Moderato
mf

C. FRANCK
Domine non secundum

93 Andante non troppo
p

G. LANGE (1830-1889)
Arietta - Sonatina Op. 114 n. 4

94 Andantino
mf

M. HAYDN
Wie trostreich

L.E. GEBHARDI
Morgengesang

L.E. GEBHARDI
Wasserlied

34

L.E. GEBHARDI
Der Sommerabend

A. SCHMOLL
En prière

F. BURGMÜLLER (1806-1874)
Ave Maria

FINGERING CHART

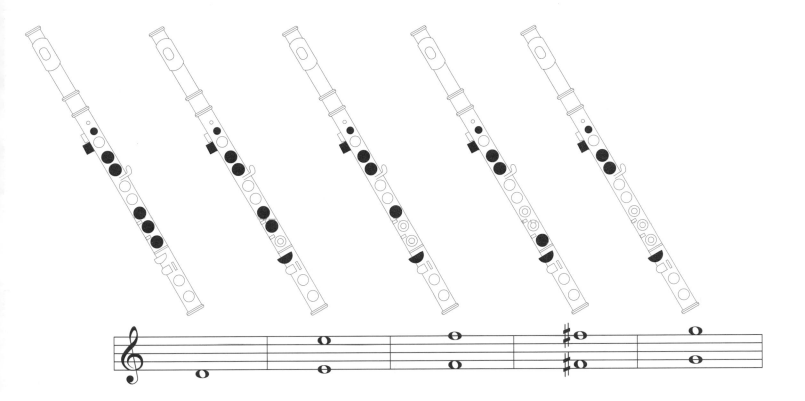

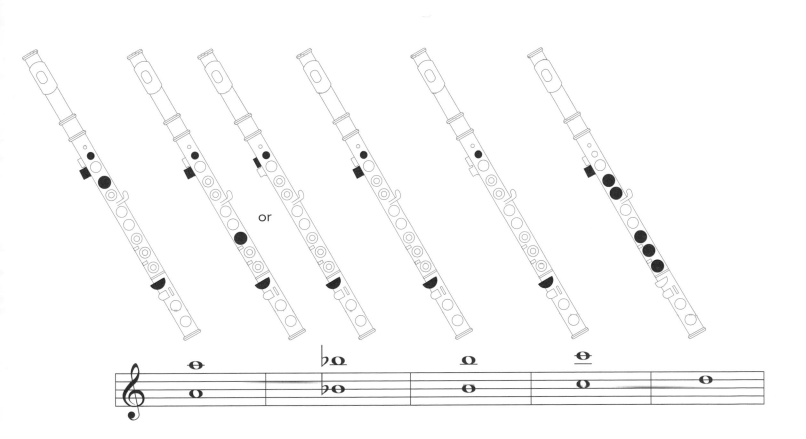

GLOSSARY

A tempo giusto	*In strict tempo*
Adagio religioso	*Slow, devotional*
Allegretto	*Fairly quick*
Allegro	*Fast*
Allegro moderato	*Moderately fast*
Andante	*Walking tempo*
Andante con moto	*Walking tempo with motion*
Andante moderato	*Moderate walking tempo*
Andante non troppo	*Walking tempo not too much*
Andantino	*Close to walking tempo*
Animato	*Animatedly*
Assai vivo	*Very lively*
Brillante e vivace	*Brilliant and lively*
Comodo	*Comfortably*
Con moto	*With motion*
Larghetto	*A little broad*
Largo	*Broad*
Lento	*Slow*
Maestoso ma non lento	*Majestic but not slow*
Melodioso	*Singing*
Menuetto grazioso	*Graceful minuet*
Moderato	*Moderately*
Molto allegro	Very quick
Non troppo veloce	*Not too rapidly*
Presto	*Very fast*
Un poco animato	*A little animated*
Vivace	*Lively*